A
SIMPLE PATH
TO
FOLLOWING
JESUS

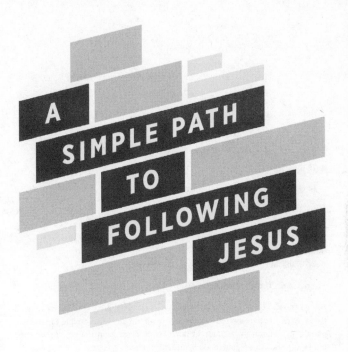

A SIMPLE PATH TO FOLLOWING JESUS

RUSTY GEORGE

BETHANYHOUSE

a division of Baker Publishing Group
Minneapolis, Minnesota

© 2020 by Rusty George

Published by Bethany House Publishers
11400 Hampshire Avenue South
Bloomington, Minnesota 55438
www.bethanyhouse.com

Bethany House Publishers is a division of
Baker Publishing Group, Grand Rapids, Michigan

Printed in the United States of America

ISBN 978-0-7642-3792-8

Unless otherwise indicated, Scripture quotations are from the Holy Bible, New
International Version®. NIV®. Copyright © 1973, 1978, 1984, 2011 by Biblica,
Inc.™ Used by permission of Zondervan. All rights reserved worldwide. www
.zondervan.com

The content of this book is a revised and condensed version of *Justice. Mercy. Humility.* by Rusty George.

Cover design by Greg Jackson, Thinkpen Design, Inc.

Author represented by The Gates Group

20   21   22   23   24   25   26   7   6   5   4   3   2   1

Contents

Introduction

Congratulations!

You just took a huge step in your life by deciding to follow Jesus.

Jesus said that whoever puts their trust in him will have eternal life.[1] Maybe you signified that by praying to ask Jesus to be the leader and forgiver of your life. Maybe you made a confession before others and said, "I believe Jesus is the Christ, the Son of God."[2] And maybe you followed that up by being baptized into him.[3] At this point, we begin to wonder one thing . . .

Now what?

How do you follow someone you've never met or seen, or have yet to have a conversation with?

Is it even possible to be like Jesus?

What does being a part of the church have to do with this?

Over the course of this book, I want to show you how. Simple. Memorable. Doable.

I think you'll discover that following Jesus may not always be easy . . . but it's not complicated.

CHAPTER 1

Where's the Fine Print?

EVER WONDER IF THE DECISION TO FOLLOW JESUS comes with some fine print?

Like those medications you see advertised on television:

*May cause anxiety, depression, an itch on your back you can't reach, fear of clowns, running with scissors, barking at the moon, and an unhealthy obsession with fire.

Obviously I'm exaggerating, but you get the point. Is choosing Jesus similar in that after making the decision to follow him, you're waiting for the fine print? "By the way, now you need to . . ."

*love others, forgive those who hurt you, pray for those who persecute you, have joy, be patient, stay faithful, be gentle with your words, give to the hurting, tithe, live in peace, go to church every week, serve in your church, read your Bible every day, pray without ceasing, be kind to everyone on the freeway, don't drink, don't smoke, don't go with girls who do, and confess your sins every night, for if you don't, you might wake up in hell!

We don't know what to do with all the things in the Bible that seem to be necessary, so we make them into a to-do list. Then we treat them as the way to get God's attention and favor.

For centuries, we've been trying to figure out how to get God's attention. And not only get his attention, but also his approval. It has driven some to exhaustion, others to disbelief, and some nearly mad. Is this really what Jesus intended when he said, "Follow me"? Is this what God had in mind when he said, "You will be my people and I will be your God"?

Sometimes people do seemingly crazy things to live out the fine print.

Cain and Abel had to be the first. They were the sons of Adam and Eve. They grew up outside of Eden and had never known what it was like to have walked with God in the cool of the day like their parents had. So getting God's attention and gaining his favor was something that was not only new to them, but also something they sought to attain. They each prepared offerings to be presented to God, but someone went cheap. Abel brought a gift that was both extravagant and intentional; Cain brought leftovers. Abel brought meat; Cain brought grain. (Is this proof that God is not a vegetarian?) Whatever the case, Abel's sacrifice was accepted and Cain's was not—telling us very early on that there are right ways and wrong ways to try to connect with God.

The tower of Babel comes next. Was it pride or was it passion that caused these foolhearted people to decide to build a tower toward heaven? They wanted to make a name for themselves. They wanted to touch the sky. They wanted to be God-like in their presence and notoriety. Was this an attempt at immortality? At any rate, the metaphor is rather pronounced as an effort to be noticed by man, disguised as a method to reach God.

Fast-forward to the New Testament and you see the Pharisees taking things up a notch. They received the Old Testament law and made it their priority to be close to God. They kept the laws and then some. They had laws to keep the laws to keep the laws. These guys were the masters of overkill. No one would utter the name of God—Yahweh—so they shortened it to "Ya" (thus, Hallelu–Ya, or Hallelujah). When writing that name, they would write a letter and go wash themselves, then write another letter, repeat. I'm sure they were grateful God's name was not Rumpelstiltskin. The problem with their way of life is they were so focused on the law of God they couldn't see the Son of God when he arrived.

This strange collection of efforts doesn't end there.

In AD 400 we learn about a man named St. Simeon, who was rather extreme as well. He joined a monastery at the age of sixteen, but even this proved to be too worldly, so he shut himself in a hut for three years and went the entire time of Lent without eating or drinking. After this, he moved to the desert to "imprison" himself in a small cave. But too many people sought him out, asking him to pray for them, so he finally decided to withdraw as much as he could. He had a pillar erected fifty feet in the air, where he built a small platform and decided to live out his days up there in communion with God until his death. He stayed on the pillar for thirty-six years. And you thought the Sunday service was long. . . .[1]

Creative and painful ways to connect with God are not found only in the past, but also in the present. A man named Carl James Joseph from Detroit, Michigan, hit nationwide news when he began dressing like Jesus and carrying a cross down the street. Carl, referred to as the Catholic Pilgrim from Detroit, has been living without money and depending on the generosity of others for twenty years. Because of all this, he has been given the nickname "The Jesus Guy." The Jesus Guy has now visited over twenty countries and has become a well-known figure in the old city of Jerusalem. When asked about his choice to do this, he states he simply wants to emulate his Lord.[2]

So is that what it takes to follow Jesus?

Around 730 BC, we are given a phrase from the prophet Micah who was trying to get God's people to follow God again. They were God's people, his royal priesthood, a holy nation, blessed to be a blessing, but they were living below their calling. They were consumed with hedonism, selfishness, and idol worship. They would drift into pits of despair, were obsessed with self-preservation, and wallowed in their own fears and misfortune. It is into this setting that the prophet Micah is called to bring a word of realignment.

I wonder if you need to hear those words. Perhaps you are stuck in what seems to be an endless cycle of selfishness, despair, self-preservation, and exhaustion. Perhaps you know what it's like to be stuck in the performance trap of religious perfectionism. Maybe you're wondering if there is another list you've missed or another scorecard to fill out. What does it really take to get God's attention, to stay in God's good graces, and to live a life in the center of his will and blessing?

The prophet Micah gives Israel words that will be overlooked and passed over, but fortunately, passed on. And we learn what God does look at, how God does judge the heart, and what we should focus on. It's not another set of tasks to add to our already growing religious to-do list; rather, it's a statement that encapsulates the heart of God.

Justice, mercy, humility. Three words that can change everything.

Granted, following Jesus is not always easy, but it was never meant to be complicated.

CHAPTER 2

What about All the Rules?

IN THE BEGINNING, IT STARTED WITH ONE RULE: Don't eat of the tree. That didn't end so well. #epicfail. Then it turned into ten rules, i.e., the Ten Commandments. The Israelites failed one of those even before Moses could bring them down the mountain. After that, it was a colossal mess of breaking rules and offering sacrifices for forgiveness. The Pharisees enacted over six hundred laws just to help us all keep the original ten. That was pretty overwhelming.

And then Jesus comes around and reduces it all to two:

"Teacher, which is the greatest commandment in the Law?" Jesus replied, "'Love the Lord your God with all your heart and with all your soul and with all your mind.' This is the first and greatest commandment. And the second is like it: 'Love your neighbor as yourself.' All the Law and the Prophets hang on these two commandments."

Matthew 22:36–40

Love God. Love people. That seems easier than remembering six hundred commands.

Fast-forward a few months and Jesus makes it even simpler. While seated around the table for his last meal with his disciples, Jesus says,

> "A new command I give you: Love one another. As I have loved you, so you must love one another."
>
> John 13:34

He reduces it all down to one thing: How you love people shows how you love God. In other words, "You want to love my Father? Love his kids."

I know this is true for me. You can be kind to me and flatter me all day long, but if you aren't nice to my kids, then we are not all right. And our heavenly Father reduces everything down to this one thing: You show how you love me by how you love what I love . . . and I love people.

This really goes against the popular sayings of "I love Jesus, just not his friends," or, "My faith is private; I love God and forget about the rest." Jesus says we can't love his Father without loving his kids. It's that simple.

When Jesus said to love God and love people, he said all the Law and the Prophets hang on these two commands; now he is saying, "You know what? It really all hinges on loving people." Everything from Genesis to the maps . . . it all is about loving people.

If you do this, you not only love people, you also show your love of God. Everything hinges on this one thing.

That's a big deal to our heavenly Father, and it should be to us.

But how?

How do I love people? Just be nice? Smile more? How about I let people cut in front of me in line. How many cars should I let go before me—one? Two? What does loving people look like?

It looks the same way that Jesus loved people.

For most of us, we think this might be unattainable. After all, I can't heal people, forgive sins, or speak words people will never forget. The closest to being like Jesus I think I can do is wear sandals. Maybe grow a beard.

But Jesus would have lived with a simple motto in his head. Being raised Jewish, he would have known the Law and the Prophets, and certainly he would have been taught this refrain from the prophet Micah some seven hundred years before he sets foot on the earth.

The hidden gem in Micah's prophecy is that he tells the wayward people how to return to God. He gives them the process of what it would take to have prayers answered, questions make sense, and God's favor rest upon them once again. This ancient document was saved, preserved, and revered years later . . . but was ignored in its day. And this ancient document not only clearly states how to return to God, it also sets up the road map for how to follow his Son, who will arrive seven hundred years later.

Micah starts off with describing our predicament. How will we get right with God?

> With what shall I come before the LORD and bow down before the exalted God? Shall I come before him with burnt offerings, with calves a year old? Will the LORD be pleased with thousands of rams, with ten thousand rivers of olive oil? Shall I offer my firstborn for my transgression, the fruit of my body for the sin of my soul?

> Micah 6:6–7

The word *exalted* simply means "heights." He asks, "How do we come before this God who is so high above us?" Isn't that how we feel in our daily lives? We are so thick in the routine of to-do lists, carpool schedules, soccer tournaments, project reviews, dentist appointments, and homework that we think, *God is so high above this.* He's on another level. He sees all and deals with all. He's managing the cosmos, the climate, the continents, and the Kardashians. . . . How does he see my busy little life? How would I even get his attention? How would I just get in good with him, let alone haveh a relationship with him? So our natural reaction is theirs . . . a big, gaudy sacrifice.

For them, that might be burnt offerings, young calves, herds of rams, or maybe rivers of oil. What about the Canaanite practice of sacrificing your firstborn? While we may not think that extreme, for us it might be six weeks in a row at church—taking notes. Maybe it's finally giving some money in the offering plate. Perhaps it's doing a Beth Moore Bible study or deciding to keep a prayer journal. Maybe it's trying to stop swearing, drinking less, or staying off certain websites. "Oh, I know, what if for the next thirty days, every post I make on social media is a Bible verse?" Certainly these things will get God's attention. Certainly these might make God grant me my request, or at least lay off the punishment I feel I may have coming.

That's the way the Israelites thought. Yet Micah says it's so much simpler.

He sums it up this way:

> He has shown you, O mortal, what is good. And what does the Lord require of you? To act justly and to love mercy and to walk humbly with your God.

> Micah 6:8

Justice. Mercy. Humility. That's it.

Seriously? What's the catch? Where's the fine print?

Everything God has told us to do can be summed up in this statement. Everything God was asking the nation of Israel to be can be summed up in three words. The family of Abraham, the call to be a blessing, the Ten Commandments, the creeds of the Judges, the cries of the prophets, and eventually the call to follow Jesus all come down to act justly, love mercy, and walk humbly with our God. Justice. Mercy. Humility.

So what does that mean?

Over the next few chapters we'll see how Jesus lived this out, what it means to follow Jesus and love people, and thus what it means to find our purpose in life.

CHAPTER 3

Act Justly

WHEN WE THINK OF ACTING JUSTLY, WE TEND TO THINK OF HELPING THE DOWN AND OUT, those who are in a tough spot, and those who can't stand up for themselves. The question is: What is "just" enough?

When my wife and I first moved to California, we were invited by some locals to try a Los Angeles landmark known for their French dip sandwiches. In fact, they even claimed to have invented them. (Wouldn't it then be called an L.A. dip sandwich? What do I know?) Philippe's is located in downtown L.A., and it took us about an hour to get there. We exited the freeway and began weaving through the concrete jungle of the inner city, passing cardboard houses and panhandlers on the corner. As we pulled into the parking lot and opened the car doors, the smell of roast beef and freshly baked bread greeted us and called us inside. I could already tell this would be worth the drive.

Making our way to the front door, we were approached by a homeless man. He asked if we had any money we might

21

be able to give him. He was trying to get a bus ticket back to his family in Kentucky. I can be a bit skeptical at times with people's stories. Why was he headed to Kentucky? What would he actually do with the money? I suspiciously began to ask him some questions about where his family in Kentucky lived. We had lived there for several years and I might be able to validate his story. But before I could finish my investigation, one of our friends pulled out a twenty-dollar bill and handed it to him. The gentleman was very grateful and then walked over and hopped on a very nice bicycle and road off down the road. This was a bit unsettling for my friend, who had just ponied up a twenty. "Where'd he get the bike?" he wondered out loud. "Is he really going to Kentucky?" I began to nod in agreement with his concerns, and then just before one of us said, "I bet he's going to use the money for drugs and alcohol," one of the ladies we were with spoke up. "Who cares what he does with it? That's on him. It was on you to give him the money!" I felt a bit ashamed that I didn't say that. After all, I'm the pastor in the group. But as right as she was, is that all I could have done?

Is giving someone a twenty-dollar bill truly living out justice, mercy, and humility? Or is it just charity?

What does it mean to act justly? Is it to defend those who are struggling? Is it to protect those who are vulnerable? Maybe you think of a noble hero who opened a soup kitchen, or a family who took in foster kids, or maybe an organization fighting to end human trafficking.

Simply put: Justice is to give others what they deserve.

That may be money, that may be resources, but often it is dignity.

Jesus addressed this in his haunting story about the sheep and the goats as recorded in Matthew 25. Speaking of the hungry, sick, and alien, Jesus says, "Truly I tell you, whatever you did for one of the least of these brothers and sisters of mine, you did for me" (Matthew 25:40).

Food, shelter, clothing . . . yes. But more than that, Jesus says, "I was lonely and you stayed with me." What if the greatest resource we can provide costs us nothing but our time? And what if the gift of a listening ear is more valuable to someone than a twenty-dollar bill?

In the Gospels, we read that Jesus often "sent out" his disciples to do ministry: "He sent them out to proclaim the kingdom of God and to heal the sick" (Luke 9:2; see also Luke 10:9). Jesus talked a lot about the kingdom of God, but he wasn't just talking about another political power or government. When Jesus talks about the kingdom of God, he's referring to another way of living within the world, one that promotes peace, justice, and equality for all.

This really shows when Jesus did healings of his own. Whether he was healing a demonized person, sick person, blind person, lame person, ritually unclean person, or the like, they received more than a physical healing; he was healing them spiritually and restoring them to access to the very community from which they were outcast because of their various conditions. Jesus saw people for who they were—children of God created in his image—and simply reminded them of that fact through healing them and restoring their ability to make an impact on the community around them.

Furthermore, Jesus calls his church to do the very same. One of the first descriptions we see of the early church after Jesus ascended into heaven was that "there were no needy persons among them" (Acts 4:34). This is a mirror image of what God was calling Israel to do in Deuteronomy 15:4 as we read earlier.

"The goal is to see people restored to being what God created them to be: people who understand that they were created in the image of God with the gifts, abilities, capacity to make decisions and to effect change in the world around them; and people who steward their lives, communities, resources, and relationships in order to bring glory to God."[1]

Offer what they need most. Dignity.

It's a shame, but when many of us are moved to "give to the poor," we do so under the motivation of making those to whom we're giving more like us. In other words, we think that being generous to people is to make them more middle class on an economic level. But faith requires us to change this perspective. What we can learn from Israel, as we're about to see, is that it is all about restoring a relationship. The mission and role of the church in the world today is simple: to do what Jesus did. Or put another way, to do justice, love mercy, and walk humbly with God. This seems simple enough, but it is so incredibly difficult because it requires an entire lifestyle of dedication and an entire lifetime of commitment to other people. It is so much more than a one-time donation. And particularly in North America, where capitalism is what most any of us know best, it can require a major change in how we view and describe justice and poverty.

Rodney Stark, well-known sociologist of religion, documents that the early church's engagement with suffering people was crucial to its explosive growth. Cities in the Roman Empire were characterized by poor sanitation, contaminated water, high population densities, open sewers, filthy streets, unbelievable stench, rampant crime, collapsing buildings, and frequent illnesses and plagues. Life expectancy at birth was less than thirty years—probably substantially less. "Rather than fleeing these urban cesspools, the early church found its niche there. Stark explains that the Christian concept of self-sacrificial love of others, emanating from God's love for them, was a revolutionary concept to the pagan mind, which viewed the extension of mercy as an emotional act to be avoided by rational people. Hence, paganism provided no ethical foundation to justify caring for the sick and destitute, who were being trampled by the teeming urban masses."[2]

"Christianity revitalized life in Greco-Roman cities by providing new norms and new kinds of social relationships able to cope with many urgent urban problems. To cities filled with the homeless and impoverished, Christianity offered charity as well as hope. To cities filled with newcomers and strangers, Christianity offered an immediate basis for attachments. To cities filled with orphans and widows, Christianity provided a new and expanded sense of family. To cities torn by violence and ethnic strife, Christianity offered a new basis for social solidarity. And to cities faced with epidemics, fires, and earthquakes, Christianity offered effective nursing services."[3]

I have yet to meet anyone experiencing homelessness who told me that was their plan. In most cases, their situation is a result of broken relationships rather than a lack of resources. When we see them as a person with a story, with a history, and who is often wanting someone to merely look them in the eyes and truly see them and give them a smile, recognizing them as a fellow human being, this simple act can be life-giving. If you feel compelled to give them some money, go ahead. If you have time to have coffee or share a meal, do that. Maybe you just have time to shake their hand and engage in a quick conversation. All of these actions offer more than a handout; they offer dignity.

When we engage in genuine relationships, change happens on both sides! Real transformation happens.

Jesus' plan for this to be lived out was within the context of the church. When you engage with a local church, you are partnered with other people moving ahead to advance justice in the world. Decide to join a group to go on a mission trip or do a service project at your church. This will help you take this step of acting justly.

CHAPTER 4

Love Mercy

IF ACTING JUSTLY IS TO GIVE PEOPLE WHAT THEY DESERVE, loving mercy is to give people what they don't deserve.

What is mercy?

As a kid, there was a simple rule when roughhousing and wrestling with friends. If you are clearly beat, if you are pinned to the ground, if someone is asserting their will on you in some childish yet painful way, the way to get them to stop was to yell "Mercy!" Some would say uncle, but that never made sense to me. What does my uncle have to do with it? Our safe word was mercy. And it was always honored.

Growing up, we learn that mercy is the ceasing of pain. So what does Micah mean when he says God's call for us is to "love mercy"?

At first glance, we may think that to love mercy is simply to approve of mercy. Or to cheer it on. A teacher gives a late paper a second chance, a boss gives a single mom an unexpected bonus, or a police officer gives you just a warning. We love that kind of mercy. Every now and then we hear of a tragic story of a tourist in a foreign land being arrested or detained. Our government goes to work on their behalf, and we are happy when we see their release. The news covers it as we watch their tearful return home and reunion with loved ones. We nod. We approve. We may even tear up. Mercy was given.

The stories can even be closer to home. Maybe you've seen a team member at work given a reprieve after a failed project, and they are allowed to keep their job. Perhaps you've seen a friend forgive an ex-spouse for years of infidelity and you celebrate with them. Even with our children, when their teacher lets them make up a test, or when our kids grant mercy to one another for a disparaging remark or a clear violation, we "love mercy."

But is mercy more than that?

The word Micah uses for "mercy" here is *hesed*. It's best summed up as *lovingkindness*. This was a term that was used to describe God's kindness extended to his people, and thus the kindness his people are to extend to each other. But is that it?

What I find interesting is that most translations refer to it as "steadfast love." This is often aligned with the Greek word *agape*, which is an unconditional love. The best English translation is probably "faithfulness" or "commitment."

Mercy depicts what we think of when we see how God deals with his children, the Israelites. They cry out because they are enslaved, and he delivers them. Mercy. They complain because he brought them to the Red Sea and they were about to die, and God parted the sea. Mercy. They complained because they had nothing to eat. He gave them manna every morning. Mercy. They get bored with the sweet-bread, so he gives them quail. Mercy. This is the kind, faithful, unconditional mercy that *hesed* encapsulates.

In fact, in the Old Testament, the word *hesed* is used most often for two relational situations: Those you know, and those you don't know.

And it turns out there is a big difference between how we extend this type of kind, faithful mercy based on the nature of our relationships. But it's important we extend it to both those we know and those we don't. "The refugee in Syria doesn't benefit more if you conserve your kindness only for her and withhold it from your neighbor who's going through a divorce."[1]

For Those We Don't Know

These are people we come across and have no reason to necessarily be generous or merciful to them. There is no prior relationship between you and them, but you nevertheless act generously or mercifully by remaining faithful or committed to them. It's a five-dollar bill to the guy on the corner with a cardboard sign, or letting someone go in front of you at the stop sign. You don't know them, they probably won't ever repay you, but you give them this gift of mercy. Or in another word . . . you give them the same kind of mercy and grace the children of Israel—and even the people who weren't part of the nation of Israel—received from God over and over again.

Even though God "knows" all, in the Old Testament, his covenant was only with the nation of Israel, yet you see him extending mercy to those not in this tribe. Most notably is Rahab. Here is a woman who lives in Jericho, a city that God has just instructed the Israelites to wipe out. They were an abomination to God and to his people. Rahab is not only a citizen of this place, she is also a prostitute. (Another character we did not have a flannelgraph for in my Sunday school.) Yet when Joshua and Caleb come to town to scout out the city, she gives them safe passage and hides them till they can safely escape. So God grants her his mercy. When the Israelites storm the city, she is spared. *Hesed* . . . for those who are not part of our tribe.

For Those We Know

These are our friends. Our family. Our co-workers. Our crazy cousin and the brother-in-law of whom we do not speak. We know these people, we work with these people, we even like some of these people. And sometimes they are in need of help, encouragement, assistance, or even forgiveness. Perhaps they have hurt us or betrayed us in some way. Maybe they owe us an apology they've yet to give for a car they totaled or a Christmas vacation they ruined. Whatever the case, if in spite of what they owe you, you refuse to let them end the relationship, and if you grant them kind, faithful, recurring mercy, that's the type of generosity God has modeled for us in his relationship with the Israelites.

God not only grants this to the nation of Israel when they first leave Egyptian slavery, but he also continues this pattern over and over again through the period of the Judges.

The children of Israel were led by Moses, then by Joshua, and then by Judges appointed by God. But this begins a three-hundred-plus-year pattern of God's people disobeying, then facing the consequences, then receiving God's mercy.

> Whenever the LORD raised up a judge for them, he was with the judge and saved them out of the hands of their enemies as long as the judge lived; for the LORD relented because of their groaning under those who oppressed and afflicted them. But when the judge died, the people returned to ways even more corrupt than those of their ancestors, following other gods and serving and worshiping them. They refused to give up their evil practices and stubborn ways.
>
> Judges 2:18–19

These people had a pull toward evil. They were easily distracted and enamored by the gods of neighboring countries. Sure, these gods had never delivered their people from Egyptian rule, these gods had never parted the Red Sea, these gods had never provided manna and quail in the desert, but they did allow prostitution as acts of worship. So for some reason, these people were easily persuaded. I'm so glad that we've grown beyond that!

God would allow them to feel the full weight of his justice and their consequences, but when they would cry uncle, he would step in with mercy. Kind, faithful, and compassionate. He would rescue them and appoint a new judge to lead them. And over three centuries they would obey, then rebel, then suffer, then cry uncle, and God would use a total of fifteen judges to bring them mercy.

Time and again God continues to act justly but then show mercy. Why does he do this? Because this is who God is . . . and this is who he asks us to be.

Granting kind, faithful mercy to those who are closest to us should be easy. After all, some of these people we are talking about are loved ones. It's easy to grant mercy to our kids. We have to fight to NOT give too much mercy at times. It's easy to grant mercy to those who can bless us. For instance, most of us tend to let our boss have a pass because they sign our paychecks. We even tend to let people we *think* we know have mercy—for example, an athlete who plays for our favorite team or an actor of our favorite show. We feel like we know them, so when they make a mistake, when they miss a game-winning shot or are rude to the press, we cut them some slack because they make our lives better. Mercy to those we know or even think we know should come easy.

But not every time.

Sometimes the hardest to grant kind, faithful compassion and grace toward are those we know the best. Because no one can hurt us like a friend.

I've had acquaintances leave the church because they didn't like me or were mad at us for something we did or didn't do. And their words stung. But it's nothing compared to the words of a friend; they cut deep.

Maybe it was a trusted friend who sent a negative text about you to someone else but didn't know you were on the group chat. Your first thought is not justice or mercy, it's "ouch."

Maybe it was a co-worker who stole your ideas, took credit for your work, and got the promotion that you felt was yours. What do you say the next time you see them?

Perhaps it was a spouse. They promised forever, but then you found out they were cheating on you. When you confronted them, they were not repentant and contrite; they were harsh and distant and blamed you for their lack of love at home and the need to look elsewhere. How can you ever trust again? Mercy for them? What about the kids? Are you kidding? How about mercy for me!

The words of Micah are interesting in their translation to love mercy. It's this idea of "I want mercy for you," "I celebrate when you get mercy," and "I love to give mercy to others." But how can we do that when the one who needs it the most seemingly deserves it the least? After all, they were a trusted part of your world.

As always, Jesus models it for us best.

When Jesus first met Peter, Peter was a rough-mouthed, hard-living fisherman who had given up on religion and was pursuing the family trade. But when Jesus helps him catch more fish than he'd ever seen, Peter decides to leave it all behind and follow him. They quickly become fast friends.

Yet despite being a Jesus follower, Peter continues to say and do some pretty reckless things.

One day, Jesus is with his disciples and he asks them, "Who do you say I am?" They all hem and haw a bit with various answers, but then it is Peter who steps up and says, "You are the Messiah." Right answer, Peter! And Jesus commends him with, "On this rock I will build my church!" (Matthew 16:15–18). This is the guy who confessed early to having a dirty mouth. Jesus loves mercy.

Yet not long after this, Jesus will begin telling people of how he will soon have to die. Peter steps up, thinking he's saying the right thing, and declares, "This shall never happen!" To which Jesus says, "Get behind me, Satan!" (Matthew 16:22–23). Seems like Jesus administers some justice by putting Peter in his place!

On another occasion, Jesus will walk on water by a boat filled with the disciples. Peter will come out to join Jesus. But after taking a few steps, he starts to sink. Jesus helps him. Mercy. Jesus corrects him: "Why did you doubt?" (Matthew 14:31). Justice.

The most memorable of all is the time when Peter denies Jesus outside in the courtyard near where Jesus is on trial. Three times people claim Peter knew Jesus, and three times Peter says,

"I never knew him." After the resurrection, Jesus and Peter have some unfinished business. Justice, if you will. And sure enough, Jesus asks Peter a piercing question: "Do you love me?" What makes this so painful is he asks it three times—one for each denial. Peter responds yes each time, but the justice has been clear. Then, in a strange twist, Jesus commissions Peter back with his original calling: build the church. Or "feed my sheep." Mercy. (See Matthew 26:34; Mark 14:30; Luke 22:34.)

Jesus is modeling how mercy can put a nuance on justice. We act justly so we can show mercy. God wants us to act decisively in a way that shows faithfulness to people just as God does to us.

What can we learn from Jesus on how to show mercy to those we trust the most and thus hurt us the most?

Mercy Is Not Commending

At no point does Jesus say, "What you did was right," or even, "I get it, we all make mistakes." He acknowledges what was wrong. He calls it out. Then he offers mercy. You can still play in my sandbox.

Mercy Is Not Forgetting

Jesus had not forgotten what Peter had done. He addressed it. And then moved on. Granting mercy to someone in your life allows the relationship to continue, but it may take time for you to forget what happened. If ever. A wife who forgives her husband for an affair is merciful enough to allow the marriage to continue, but will find it hard to forget what has happened. And while the Father, Son, and Holy Spirit are able to forget, we may not be able to. Jesus models for us here that sometimes it's good to remember so we can address it and deal with the grievance.

Mercy Is Not Just for Their Sake

When you grant someone mercy, it always impacts more than just the person who receives it. Sometimes the recipient is you. Even though you have let them off the hook by giving mercy, you feel a weight lifted because you are not carrying this weight anymore. It can be exhausting to always be reminding yourself who you are mad at and why. Letting that burden go can be life-giving to you as well.

In some ways, mercy is like forgiveness. But while forgiveness is more of a legal term, like saying, "You don't owe me anymore. Paid in full," mercy is more like a medical term: "Let me offer healing for what it is you have done."

Sometimes the recipient is you; sometimes it's for others unrelated to your issue. In Peter's case, he received mercy, but the beneficiary was more than just him. It was the church. Because of this mercy and recommissioning from Jesus, he was able to stand up in front of thousands on the day of Pentecost and preach the gospel, and the church was born. This mercy was multiplied to countless others. We never know how the mercy we extend will impact more than just those immediately involved.

In a sentence, to love mercy is to extend kindness and compassion whether they deserve it or not.

So let's get started. To whom do you need to give mercy? A friend who has disappointed you? A family member who has let you down? A co-worker who has offended you? Or maybe it's yourself. Maybe you're the one who needs to be shown mercy. Whoever it is, the quicker you say, "I'm letting you out of jail," the quicker you'll be set free.

Free people find their future.

The church is to be a place of freed people helping others find freedom. Take the time to invite a friend to join you on your journey at your church.

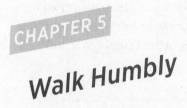

CHAPTER 5

Walk Humbly

FOLLOWING JESUS IS TO OFFER JUSTICE AND MERCY, BUT TO DO SO IN A SPIRIT OF HUMILITY. So Micah concludes his edict with, "Walk humbly with your God" (Micah 6:8).

In a world of social media posts where we seem to all be yelling "Look at me!" it sometimes feels like humility might have gotten lost. Humility is not just thinking less of yourself, so let's start with what humility is NOT:

Self-deprecating

When we talk of walking humbly with our God, the reflex is to lean toward self-deprecation. *I am nothing. I am worthless. He is worthy. He is holy. We are not.*

The assumption is that we need to emphasize our weaknesses, joke about our insecurities, and highlight our faults. But just because we talk down about ourselves doesn't mean we stop thinking about ourselves. Often it can be just the opposite.

The flip side of arrogance is self-deprecation. Two sides to the same pride coin. When we're obsessed with our nothingness, our shortcomings, or our inadequacies, we're still obsessed with our self.

Quiet

It's funny how we are often quick to assume that quiet people are humble. But in reality, we don't know what is going through their minds as they sit silently. They could be thinking how stupid we all are and how they shouldn't waste their breath on us.

I once knew a very talented musician. He led his church in worship every weekend, and to the onlooker it appeared this leader was incredibly humble. He sang, he encouraged from stage, and he was quiet all the time. Everyone assumed his silence off-stage was due to him being in deep communion with the Lord, and when on stage we were witnessing their relationship in action. So when this worship leader left the church to go to another, we all assumed the church would take a dive. After all, the spiritual divining rod was moved. But when this worship leader left, the church didn't tank as many assumed; it took off. I asked a seasoned pastor what he thought the reason was, and his answer was simple: "Pride has left the building." I was a bit stunned and asked what he meant. "He was arrogant. Just because you're quiet doesn't mean you can't think highly of yourself. Now that pride has left, the Holy Spirit has room to work again."

Encouraging

There are some phrases in the church that quickly become associated with spiritual depth. For instance:

"Lord willing, I'll see you next week," which means, "I plan on being here next week, but it's up to God."

"We pray a hedge of protection around you and for Satan to be bound," which means, "I pray that your plans are successful."

"Travel mercies for you," which means, "I hope you get there safely."

Seemingly humble people have similar expressions:

"It was a team effort." This is what humble people say when they are given credit for doing a good job. They deflect to the team.

"God gets all the glory." Another phrase used often when someone says, "Great job." You can hear this everywhere from the church lobby to the Grammys.

"Bless your heart." This seems to be genuine and kind,
but everyone from the South knows this just means
"You're an idiot."

People who say kind, encouraging, and positive words
to others often appear to be humble. And they may be. But
being an encouraging person is not a pathway toward walking in humility. Encouraging is a *result* of being humble at
heart.

As mentioned in the last chapter, Micah's goal for us is
to walk with God in such a way that we are awed by who
he is. The focus is all on God. Not on our arrogance or our
deprecation.

And to go along with what was recorded in many entries
in the book of Proverbs, the result of our humility is wisdom.
Often, wisdom does not simply come from adding deprecation, shyness, or encouragement to our repertoire.

Typically, we look at how Jesus did this so we can understand how to follow him, but in this case, let's look at his
cousin John, the baptizer—aka John the Baptist. John was
born before Jesus and was said to be the "forerunner" or
predecessor to clear the way for Jesus. Judging by his adult
behavior of living as a recluse in the wilderness, eating locusts and honey, we can only assume he was an interesting
child. Growing up hearing how your cousin is better than you
might do that to a person. I can imagine John out back eating
bugs off the tree while all the other children ate peanut butter
and jelly. Preaching to anyone who would listen. Sizing up

the family dog for a possible outfit. It came as no shock to his parents when he decided to pack up his sandwich board and head out to the Wild West.

This was a guy who was comfortable with people thinking less of him. He was at ease with people calling him crazy. But is that humility? Confidence in your insanity isn't necessarily a virtue.

Yet John seems to have something figured out when it comes to his proper place with Jesus.

> Now this was John's testimony when the Jewish leaders in Jerusalem sent priests and Levites to ask him who he was. He did not fail to confess, but confessed freely, "I am not the Messiah." They asked him, "Then who are you? Are you Elijah?" He said, "I am not." "Are you the Prophet?" He answered, "No" (John 1:19–21).

John is pretty adamant about who he is not. He refuses to accept any title that is not his. He is not the Messiah, he is not even a prophet. But no self-deprecation, because he does know who he is.

> Finally they said, "Who are you? Give us an answer to take back to those who sent us. What do you say about yourself?" John replied in the words of Isaiah the prophet, "I am the voice of one calling in the wilderness, 'Make straight the way for the Lord.'" Now the Pharisees who had been sent questioned him, "Why then do you baptize if you are not the Messiah, nor Elijah, nor the Prophet?" "I baptize

with water," John replied, "but among you stands one you do not know. He is the one who comes after me, the straps of whose sandals I am not worthy to untie."

John 1:22–27

I know exactly who I am. I know my place. I know my role. And I simply announce his arrival.

There is something that is freeing about knowing who you are and who you are not. It must be the way a baseball pitcher must feel about his batting skills. Greg Maddux is one of the greatest pitchers of all time, but his batting average was a dismal .171. But no one ever told him that if he would just work on his batting, he could really be something someday. In fact, he didn't even have the greatest arm. Greg Maddux never "lit up the gun," but he knew exactly what pitch to throw and where to place it, and it drove hitters nuts. None of his coaches ever said, "Throw it over ninety-five miles an hour, and THEN you'll REALLY be something!" He already WAS something—a Hall of Fame pitcher! Similar to this, knowing who we are in Christ and for Christ helps us understand how we walk in humility. As John said, "I am the voice. . . . 'Make straight the way for the Lord'" (John 1:23).

His resolve is so strong that he is even content to lose fans and followers.

The next day John was there again with two of his disciples. When he saw Jesus passing by, he said, "Look, the Lamb of God!" When the two disciples heard him say this, they followed Jesus.

John 1:35–37

It's at this point in John's life that he has prepared for Jesus, baptized Jesus, and now keeps pointing people to Jesus. And each time he does, his crowd gets smaller; people leave him to follow Jesus, and he is fine with that. That's humility. Notice John does not say, "I'm a fool. Follow him." He just says, "There he is. The one I exist to serve." And when others follow Jesus, it not only fulfills Jesus' call, it fulfills John's mission. Everyone wins when we are humble.

John emphasizes this when someone comes to him with this news.

They came to John and said to him, "Rabbi, that man who was with you on the other side of the Jordan—the one you testified about—look, he is baptizing, and everyone is going to him" (John 3:26).

This would be the same as someone telling you that everyone is leaving your restaurant and going down the street. Or in my case, everyone is leaving your church and going down the street. Isn't there something in you that says, "Wait a minute!" I know there is in me. But not John.

To this John replied, "A person can receive only what is given them from heaven. You yourselves can testify that I said, 'I am not the Messiah but am sent ahead of him.'"

John 3:27–28

This was not my crowd to begin with. They always belonged to him.

How do you know when you are humble? Not when you are quiet or even self-deprecating, but when you are joyful that others get credit. Especially when it's God.

And then John says something that puts all of this in perspective and yet is often misunderstood:

"He must become greater; I must become less."

John 3:30

The emphasis here is that Jesus is already great but must be lifted up. Exalted. Made famous. None of us would argue with this. All of John's ministry will be spent to make this happen. John prepared the way for him, even baptized him upon Jesus' own direction, and then he kept telling people to look at Jesus . . . the Lamb of God who takes away the sin of the world. Jesus must become greater.

The next line is the one we miss. John doesn't say, "I must become nothing" or "I am nothing"; he says, "I must become less." Semantics, you say? Not necessarily. John is leaving room for himself to still be *something*. He's not nothing. He just knows who he is in comparison to Jesus. This is why self-deprecation is not always humility, or even not always needed, because in the kingdom of Jesus, the poor are rich, the meek are strong, and the persecuted are lifted up. There is still a place for us to use our gifts, play our part, and be who God has called us to be. The humility comes in knowing our role.

If there was anyone who modeled what it meant to walk in confident humility, it was Jesus. As we discussed before, take another look at how Paul describes him:

> "Have the same mindset as Christ Jesus: Who, being in very nature God, did not consider equality with God something to be used to his own advantage; rather, he made himself nothing by taking the very nature of a servant, being made in human likeness. And being found in appearance as a man, he humbled himself by becoming obedient to death—even death on a cross!"

> Philippians 2:5–10

Despite being God in the flesh, he lived as a man. He had the confidence of being King but the heart of a servant. Yet none of us would say that Jesus was not confident. This is the same Jesus who turned over the tables outside the temple, the same Jesus who asked his Father for "another way" to save the world. The same Jesus who powerfully walked through an angry mob ready to throw him off a cliff, leaving all falling on their faces around him. The same Jesus who wept at the tomb of Lazarus.

There is a parable Jesus tells that I think really drives this point home. In Luke 18:9–14, Jesus tells the parable of the

Pharisee and the tax collector. In fact, Luke says he tells this parable specifically "To some who were confident of their own righteousness and looked down on everyone else" (Luke 18:9). Basically, he says, there is a Pharisee and a tax collector, both of whom go to the temple to pray and worship. The Pharisee did all the right things, but he thanked God that he was "not like those other people." On the other hand, the tax collector is on his knees, crying to God and beating his chest, begging for forgiveness.

It's pretty easy to hear that parable and immediately apply it to someone else. The irony is, when that is our immediate response, it also automatically makes us the audience. As followers of Jesus, we are instructed to be humble, to not look down on others, and to stop categorizing people on a spiritual spectrum. Easier said than done, right? How do we get past this? How can we remain humble and not overly confident?

Maybe the first thing we need to do is remind ourselves that it is not about us. This is so counterintuitive because every waking moment is focused on seeking our own comfort or gain. "What do I want to do?" "How can I be happier?" "Where should I go to lunch?" "What's in it for me?" And the moment someone challenges this, we rise up and declare our confident spirit of inalienable rights. "I have a right to McDonald's today!" Perhaps the first thing we do is recognize, *It's not about me.*

But if that's all we do, we will become reliant on self-talk and self-flagellation to somehow stop thinking of ourselves.

We need to put the focus where Jesus did: on the One he walked with and we walk with as well—the Father.

Several years ago, I was invited by a friend to go fly-fishing in Montana. Normally I'd pass on this since I don't particularly care for fishing. But this was *fly-fishing* in *Montana*. My thoughts immediately envisioned me looking like Brad Pitt in *A River Runs Through It*. It sounded fun and it would certainly be a first for me, so I said yes. When I got to the river, I was equipped with waders and a rod and reel, and was encouraged to give it a try. Let me just say: Brad Pitt sure made it look easy! Fortunately, we were in boats with guides who were local and knew the river like the back of their hand. They had been fly-fishing longer than I had been alive. We were in good hands. So one other rookie, the guide, and I loaded up the boat and headed downstream. The guide took us right to where we needed to go; he even put the fly on my line and told me where to cast. This went on for hours. Casting, mending, reattaching the bait, trying again. It was clear that I would not be in *A River Runs Through It 2*. Finally, after hours of trying, I caught one. And it was awesome. I reeled that fish in like my family depended on it. And even though it was roughly the size of a goldfish, I held it up and took pictures for my kids. This was my moment. It was at this point that I looked at our guide and told him he was no longer needed. He could get out at the bank and I'd take it from here; I'd mastered the art of fly-fishing.

Of course I didn't. That would be ridiculous.

I think this is where humility and confidence meet. The humility comes in knowing who I am; the confidence comes in knowing whose boat I'm in.

When I walk in humility, it's clearer to see where God is leading me.

God's rescue plan for the world was for his church to advance justice and mercy . . . but the only way to do this is in a spirit of humility. Being a part of your local church is an act of humility; you can't do this alone. Decide to engage today.

CHAPTER 6

Justice. Mercy. Humility. Repeat.

HOW CAN I HELP?

Who do I need to forgive?

It's not about me.

It looks a lot like Jesus. It looks a lot like "Love others the way I have loved you."

When I choose to do this, it changes me.

It directs my attention to others who have it worse than me.

It makes me aware of those who are overlooked and in need.

It causes my heart to break for those far from God.

It forces me to pick up trash on the street, open doors for people, let people in front of me in line, and not count the items in someone's cart if I'm in the express lane.

It causes me to get involved in a local church so I can help others.

It challenges me to think about others' needs before my own.

It convicts me to stop complaining about spotty cell service and cold pizza and start sponsoring more kids in Third World countries.

It gets me off my soap-box about the need for people to use their turn signals and stop texting at the dinner table.

It makes me advocate for the poor and the enslaved.

It causes me to not take credit for what I didn't do.

I view my church as a place to serve others instead of a place to serve me.

I begin to be happy for someone who succeeds more than me.

It makes me slow down, want to listen more, and seek to understand.

It makes me prioritize things that matter.

I stop saying "I deserve . . . "

I see the good things in my life as a privilege instead of a right.

It makes me sit down and invest in others.

I walk across the street and say hi.

I use my horn less.

I love people in my church as they are, not as they should be.

I pray more because I need help to forgive.

I read my Bible more to see how Jesus loved.

I pay for the person behind me in the drive-through.

I stop complaining about everything and correcting everyone on social media.

I enjoy *now* rather than living in the past or the future.

It reminds me I'm not the center of the universe.

And oddly enough, it looks a lot like Jesus, who, by the way, IS the center of the universe.

Justice. Mercy. Humility. Repeat.

It's not always easy. But it's not complicated.

Notes

Introduction

1. See John 3:16.
2. See Romans 10:9–10.
3. See Acts 2:38; Mark 16:16.

Chapter 1 Where's the Fine Print?

1. St. Simeon Stylites the Elder, New Advent, http://www.new advent.org/cathen/13795a.htm.
2. Sara Malm, "Motor City's Messiah! Jerusalem's famous Jesus-lookalike revealed to be a Detroit preacher," *Daily Mail*, December 18, 2013, http://www.dailymail.co.uk/news/article-2525844/The-Jesus-guy-Bearded-man-familiar-sight-Jerusalem-wearing-robe-carrying-cross-revealed-Detroit-preacher.html.

Chapter 3 Act Justly

1. Rusty George, *Justice. Mercy. Humility.* (Minneapolis, MN: Bethany House Publishers, 2019), 77.

2. Steve Corbett and Brian Fikkert, *When Helping Hurts: How to Alleviate Poverty without Hurting the Poor . . . and Yourself* (Chicago: Moody Publishers, 2014).

3. Rodney Stark, *The Rise of Christianity* (Princeton, NJ: Princeton University Press, 1996), 166.

Chapter 4 Love Mercy

1. Brené Brown, *Rising Strong* (New York: Random House, 2017), 9.

Rusty George is the lead pastor of Real Life Church Ministries (RLCM) in Valencia, California. Over his seventeen years at RLCM, the church has grown to more than 7,000 people and four campuses. Rusty speaks regularly at conferences across the country, and he lives with his wife and two daughters in Santa Clarita, California.

More from Rusty George

We've made following Jesus a to-do list, but that's not what Jesus intended when he said *Follow me*. In this practical and freeing book, pastor Rusty George shares the simplicity of what God desires from us. Living a faithful life should not be a chore. George teaches how to put away our checklists and walk humbly according to God's will for our lives.

Justice. Mercy. Humility.

Discover how to satisfy your deepest needs through the power of *us*. When we learn to live in true community, we connect with God better; heal better; and overcome fears, raise families, fight temptations, and bless the world around us better. Find the fulfillment you've been looking for, and see for yourself how God uses *we* to bring out the best in *me*.

Better Together

◆ BETHANYHOUSE